CORN SNAKE

Every Detailed Thing About Corn Snake. Their Behavior, Feeding, Housing, Temperature Reproduction And How To Take Good Care Of Them

KIRK PATRICK

Table of Contents

CHAPTER ONE

INTRODUCTION

Corn snakes are intently related to rat snakes (rat snakes additionally belong to the genus Elaphe) and are also once in a while referred to as red rat snakes (especially the amelanistic color variations). They local to the southeastern United States are frequently land-living and are energetic especially at night or at dusk and dawn.

Puppy corn snakes are usually docile, quite smooth to care for and do now not get very big therefore they make a remarkable preference for beginner snake owners.

But, they're also favorites with skilled keepers due to the great array of beautiful colors and styles selective breeding has produced.

CHAPTER TWO

BEHAVIOR AND TEMPERAMENT OF CORN SNAKE

These low-key snakes permit human beings to handle them and are commonly docile. They like to burrow and hide, so a first rate-sized enclosure and unfastened substrate (lining) on the lowest is fundamental.

Like most snakes, corn snakes are outstanding get away artists, so their enclosures have to be secure. If a snake receives out of its cage it can wander off or hurt itself (and deliver a family visitor an amazing scare).

Corn snakes—once more, like maximum snakes—are carnivores. Within the wild, they stalk their prey typically thru scent in preference to sight. And after they feel threatened, specifically in the wild, they may vibrate their tail, similar to rattlesnakes, as a defense mechanism.

CHAPTER THREE

HOUSING YOUR CORN SNAKE

Selecting a stable cage is a necessity for proper corn snake care. A 20-gallon lengthy tank (an extended and shallower model of a 20-gallon tank) makes a very good-sized cage for a corn snake. It is vital to get a comfy-becoming lid that may be clamped down for this tank as well. Corn snakes will push at the lid with their noses seeking out weaknesses and tiny openings, so the in shape of the lid may be very vital.

Provide hiding spots in your corn snake. A cover field (any closed-in container like a cardboard container will do) should be supplied that is just massive enough for the snake to curl up in; if it's miles too big the snake will not experience as at ease. Portions of bark also can provide hiding spots to your snake if it is on a substrate that lets in it to burrow underneath the bark. Ideally, a hiding place needs to be had in each of the cooler and hotter ends of the enclosure. Also, offer a department for mountaineering.

CHAPTER FOUR

FEEDING CORN SNAKE

Corn snakes are carnivorous and ought to be fed frozen thawed meals. Even though they're opportunists we have discovered that mice are the nice food plan for a corn snake. A specifically massive corn snake may additionally move on to the smaller rats while absolutely grown however an all rodent weight loss program is great.

As hatchlings, corn snakes ought to be fed weekly on defrosted pinky mice, because the snake grows the meals size ought to be increased till the snake is taking massive mice or maybe jumbos. Corn snakes can be fed as soon as each two weeks as they are able to become obese if fed weekly.

extra distinct opportunity diets like gerbils, hamsters, multimammate mice or chicks can be used if the corn snake might not take something else however they are not as nutritious as the mice, it may be hard to locate them inside the length required and they aren't constantly as available.

We usually encompass a medium or big sized water bowl in the snake's enclosure. You might note the snake use it for bathing, that is commonly to cool down or to assist loosen its losing pores and skin. Both the water bowl should be stored at the cool aspect of the enclosure to prevent it from elevating the humidity inside the enclosure.

CHAPTER FIVE

REPRODUCTION OF CORN SNAKE

Corn snakes mate in both the spring and the autumn. "Men might also have interaction in ritual combat (body-shoving contests) while two or extra meet inside the presence of a receptive girl," he stated. Corn snakes are oviparous, that means that the moms lay eggs. The mom pops out 10 to 30 eggs any time from May additionally to July. She lays them in rotting stumps, and in piles of decaying plants or other places where there can be sufficient warmness and humidity for the eggs to incubate. Then, she slithers off, never to peer the babies.

The eggs gestate for about 2 months. Whilst born, babies are 10 to 15 inches (25 to 38 cm) long and are patterned like adults. Their blotches, but, are lots darker, being brown to almost black on a gray or light-orange frame.

They could live as much as 22 years in captivity, though their existence expectancy within the wild is less.

Corn snakes have slender frame which could reach 24 to 72 inches in length.

Corn snake are typically orange or dark yellow in coloration. They've purple blotches and stripes on the returned and lateral aspects of the body. Stomach is covered with black and white markings. Color of the frame depends on the habitat (it affords camouflage).

Stomach of a corn snake seems like a kernel of Indian corn, for this reason the call "corn snake". Additionally, corn snake are frequently observed close to the corn, which attracts their favored meals - rodents.

Corn snakes aren't venomous. Lamentably, people often kill corn snakes due to the fact they proportion similarities in appearance with toxic snake referred to as copperhead.

Corn snakes are diurnal animals (active in the course of the day). While they're not looking for meals, corn snakes are resting hidden in the underground burrows or beneath the rocks and bark. Corn snakes may be also seen on the trees.

Corn snakes are carnivores (meat-eaters). Younger corn snakes consume lizards and frogs, at the same time as adults hunt rodents, bats and birds and every now and then devour bird eggs.

Human beings respect corn snakes due to the fact they preserve the number of rodents under manage. Corn snakes prevent spreading of illnesses and damaging of vegetation which can be commonly associated with huge populations of rodents.

Corn snakes belong to the organization of snakes referred to as constrictors. These snakes wrap their frame across the sufferer and squeeze it till it dies out of suffocation.

Corn snakes requires meals each couple of days. As soon as the prey is dead, corn snake swallows it in one piece.

Corn snakes hibernate in the course of the cold intervals of the year.

Mating season of corn snakes generally takes area from March to can also.

Girl lays 10 to 30 eggs in the nest made from leaves or rotten wood.

Hatchlings emerge from the eggs after 65 days.

Corn snakes do now not show parental care. Infants are most effective 10 to 15 inches long at beginning and they want to fend for themselves from the primary day in their lifestyles.

Corn snakes attain sexual adulthood at the age of 18 to 36 months.

Corn snakes can survive 5 to 8 years inside the wild and up to 25 years in captivity.

CHAPTER SIX

TEMPERATURE AND HUMIDITY OF A CORN SNAKE

Obviously, corn snakes might be experiencing temperatures of around 90 of inside the solar. We attempt to offer this warmness over 1/3 of the enclosure while letting the relaxation of the enclosure cool to 70 of on the other facet. To gain this we attach a basking lamp to the ceiling of the enclosure on one side. This is controlled via a dimming thermostat to ensure that the temperature is kept correct in the course of the day. Corn snakes will be able to reach the top in their enclosure without decorations to climb on so the basking lamp needs to be surrounded by means of a guard. The basking lamp is left on for 10-12 hours according to day.

At night, all of the lighting fixtures need to burst off and the enclosure should be absolutely darkish. This have to make certain that the snake has a clear day night cycle.

Although at this point the sun has gone down, there would nevertheless be rocks, paths and roads that have warmed up in the day and in order to radiate heat for tons of the night time. To provide this warmth for the duration of the night time without introducing mild to the enclosure we lay a warmness mat underneath the basking area. The heat mat will heat items around it offering a warm patch of floor for the corn snake to relaxation on. To make certain that the warmth mat remains the suitable temperature its miles controlled via a simple on/off thermostat set to 80 of the heat mat is buried below round an inch of bedding, the sensor for the thermostat is then rested at the bedding overlaying the warmth mat in order that it may song the floor temperature of that patch of floor.

All through the day your temperatures may be lots too warm and the ceramic lamps thermostat should hold it off automatically. The heat mats will handiest start to warmth once the temperatures have dropped below 80 of at night time.

Although the thermostats we promote are very dependable it is always fine exercise to reveal your temperatures with a thermometer. A 5 of variance at the basking spot is nothing to fear approximately as long as your cool side remains cool. An easy dial thermometer on each side must be sufficient but digital probe thermometers are plenty more accurate.

CHAPTER SEVEN

PROVIDING A CLEAN ENVIRONMENT FOR YOUR CORN SNAKE

Corn snakes, as with maximum pets, require easy surroundings to thrive. We suggest a gap easy as often as viable (each day) and a full clean every 4 weeks or so. In case you are maintaining the snake in a bio-energetic enclosure you can spot smooth and monitor the enclosure. It is able to nevertheless be an excellent object to exchange out the bedding a few times in line with year.

When cleansing the enclosure you must dispose of your animal, all decorations and all of the bedding. Once the enclosure is apparent you could spray it all over with a reptile friendly disinfectant. These generally work right away and handiest need to be left for round 30 seconds, commands can commonly be observed on the disinfectants packaging. Once the disinfectant has completed its work it could be wiped away from the surfaces with a paper towel. In some instances you would possibly want to repeat this system a 2d time to make certain that the enclosure is very well cleaned.

Your decorations can be wiped clean in a similar technique, without a doubt spray them down with the disinfectant and rinse thoroughly with water earlier than drying them off and putting them lower back into the enclosure. We recommend this system is achieved all through the day time to make sure that the snake can be going again to a heat vivarium for at least an hour before the basking lamps are turned off for the night.

THE END